Avoidant *Attachment*

Workbook For Young Adults

Conquer the Fear of Closeness, Recognize Deactivation Signals, and Transition to Secure Attachment

Isabella Cruz

"Sometimes the one who's running from the life they're meant to live is the one who's running from their fears."
— Glenn Beck

Copyright   **2024 Isabella Cruz**

This book is a work of non-fiction and is based on the research and experiences of the author. Some individuals' names and personal details have been changed to protect their privacy.

Acknowledgement

I would like to extend my deepest gratitude to Dr. Read Stevenson, whose expertise as a psychiatrist has been an invaluable resource throughout the creation of this workbook. Your insights and guidance have shaped this work in profound ways.

To Dr. Jenny White, a dear friend and Clinical Psychologist, your encouragement and feedback have been both motivating and reassuring. Thank you for always being there to support me.

I am also deeply grateful to my research team, Joel and Craig, for their dedication and hard work. Your contributions have been crucial in bringing this project to life.

Finally, to my husband David and our daughter Bella, thank you for your unwavering love and support. You are my inspiration and my greatest joy.

With heartfelt thanks,

Isabella Cruz

About the Author

Isabella Cruz is a renowned psychologist and resilience coach, known for her empowering and relatable approach to mental health. Holding a doctorate in Psychology from Stanford University, she specializes in cognitive-behavioral therapy and mindfulness techniques.

With extensive experience in clinical practice, Isabella has dedicated her career to helping individuals overcome mental barriers and achieve emotional freedom. She lives in Seattle, where she continues to inspire and support others through her practice, coaching, and public speaking.

Other Books by this same author includes:

TABLE OF CONTENTS

How To Use This Workbook

Start with Self-Reflection: Begin by setting aside some quiet time to reflect on your personal experiences with attachment. This will help you connect with the material on a deeper level.

Read Each Chapter Carefully: Work through each chapter at your own pace. Take your time to understand the concepts and how they apply to your life.

Complete the Exercises: After reading, engage with the exercises provided. They are designed to help you explore your thoughts, emotions, and behaviors related to avoidant attachment.

Journal Your Thoughts: Use the space provided to jot down your thoughts, insights, and any patterns you notice as you work through the exercises.

Practice Consistently: Consistency is key. Set aside regular time each week to work on the exercises, even if it's just a few minutes a day.

Reflect and Review: Periodically, go back and review your notes and completed exercises. Reflect on your progress and how your understanding of avoidant attachment has evolved.

Apply What You Learn: Begin to apply the insights and strategies you've gained in your daily life. Notice how your relationships and interactions change as you grow.

Revisit as Needed: This workbook is a tool for ongoing growth. Feel free to revisit sections as your understanding deepens or as new challenges arise.

Introduction

Sophia had always seemed like she had everything together. She was smart, successful, and the kind of person who could walk into a room and instantly make everyone feel comfortable.

She'd been dating Ryan for about two years, and from the outside, their relationship looked perfect. They traveled together, shared inside jokes, and always seemed to be laughing. But one afternoon, out of the blue, Sophia called me, her voice shaky. She told me she had broken up with Ryan the night before.

I was shocked. Just a few weeks earlier, she'd been talking about their plans for the future—moving in together, maybe even getting married. When I asked her what had happened, she hesitated and then said, "I just wasn't feeling it anymore." It was such an unexpected answer. Sophia had never mentioned any problems, so her sudden decision didn't make sense to me.

We met up later that week at our favorite café in Capitol Hill, a cozy spot in Seattle where we often went to catch up. I could tell something was off as soon as she walked in. She looked tired, like she hadn't slept much, and she seemed distant, not her usual bubbly self.

As we sat down with our coffees, I asked her to walk me through what had happened. She started talking about how everything with Ryan had been fine, but then she began feeling suffocated. The closer they got, the more anxious she became. She said it felt like she was losing herself, and she couldn't breathe, even though Ryan hadn't done anything wrong. "He's great, really. But I just couldn't do it anymore," she said, looking down at her cup.

I listened as she talked, and it struck me that this wasn't the first time I'd heard her say something like this. In fact, it was a pattern I'd seen in her past relationships too.

Every time things started getting serious, she would pull away. I gently pointed this out to her, and at first, she shrugged it off, saying she just hadn't met the right person yet. But as we continued to talk, I could see that something was clicking for her.

I explained to Sophia about avoidant attachment, how some people develop a fear of closeness and intimacy because of past experiences, often without even realizing it. At first, she was resistant. She didn't like the idea that she might be pushing people away because of her own fears. But the more we talked, the more she started to see the connection.

She told me about how, growing up, her parents were loving but distant. They provided for her needs, but they weren't emotionally expressive, and she'd learned early on to rely on herself rather than others.

In her relationships, she had always valued her independence, but now she was beginning to see how that independence might have been a shield, keeping people at arm's length.

The turning point came a few weeks later when she called me again, this time sounding more reflective than upset. She had been thinking a lot about what we'd discussed, and she realized that her feelings of suffocation weren't about Ryan at all—they were about her own fears. She hadn't really given their relationship a chance because she was too focused on protecting herself.

Sophia decided to reach out to Ryan, not to get back together, but to explain what had happened. She wanted him to know that it wasn't about him, that she was dealing with some things she hadn't understood before.

To her surprise, Ryan was incredibly understanding. He said he had noticed her pulling away but hadn't known what to do about it. They had a long, honest conversation, and while they didn't get back together, it gave Sophia some closure and a lot to think about.

Over the next year, Sophia worked hard on understanding her attachment style. She went to therapy, read books, and started practicing being more open and vulnerable in her relationships, not just romantic ones, but with friends and family too.

She stopped seeing her independence as something that needed to be protected at all costs and started embracing the idea that it was okay to let people in.

When we met up again, almost a year later, she was in a new relationship, but this time things felt different.

She told me she still had moments of anxiety, but she wasn't running away from them anymore.

Instead, she was facing them, talking about them with her partner, and learning that it was possible to be close to someone without losing herself.

Understanding whether you have an avoidant attachment style can be an important step in your journey toward more secure and fulfilling relationships.

People with an avoidant attachment style often struggle with intimacy, preferring to keep others at a distance to protect themselves from potential emotional pain.

If you're wondering whether you might have an avoidant attachment style, this questionnaire can help you gain some clarity.

Instructions: For each statement, select the option that best describes how you generally feel in relationships.

I often find myself withdrawing from relationships when they start to become serious.
a) Strongly agree
b) Agree
c) Neutral
d) Disagree
e) Strongly disagree

I feel uncomfortable when someone tries to get emotionally close to me.
a) Strongly agree
b) Agree
c) Neutral
d) Disagree
e) Strongly disagree

I prefer to keep my personal space and independence in relationships.
a) Strongly agree
b) Agree
c) Neutral
d) Disagree
e) Strongly disagree

I find it difficult to rely on others or ask for help, even from those close to me.
a) Strongly agree
b) Agree
c) Neutral
d) Disagree
e) Strongly disagree

I sometimes feel suffocated or trapped in romantic relationships.
a) Strongly agree
b) Agree
c) Neutral
d) Disagree
e) Strongly disagree

When someone expresses their feelings for me, I often feel pressured rather than flattered.
a) Strongly agree
b) Agree
c) Neutral
d) Disagree
e) Strongly disagree

I prefer to solve my problems on my own rather than discussing them with a partner.
a) Strongly agree
b) Agree
c) Neutral
d) Disagree
e) Strongly disagree

I sometimes push people away when they get too close emotionally.
a) Strongly agree
b) Agree
c) Neutral
d) Disagree
e) Strongly disagree

I find it challenging to express my emotions or talk about my feelings.
a) Strongly agree
b) Agree
c) Neutral
d) Disagree
e) Strongly disagree

I feel more comfortable when relationships are casual rather than deeply intimate.
a) Strongly agree
b) Agree
c) Neutral
d) Disagree
e) Strongly disagree

Scoring:

- *If you selected mostly a) Strongly agree or b) Agree responses, you may have an avoidant attachment style. This means you might struggle with closeness in relationships and have a tendency to distance yourself emotionally to protect your independence.*
- *If you selected mostly c) Neutral responses, you might exhibit some avoidant tendencies, but they are not dominant in your relationships. It may be helpful to explore how these tendencies affect your interactions.*
- *If you selected mostly d) Disagree or e) Strongly disagree responses, it's likely that you do not have a predominantly avoidant attachment style. You might be more comfortable with intimacy and emotional closeness in your relationships.*

"The greatest thing you'll ever learn is just to love and be loved in return." — Eden Ahbez

Chapter 1
UNDERSTANDING AVOIDANT ATTACHMENT

Avoidant attachment isn't something we choose; it's a survival mechanism shaped by early life experiences. It's a reaction to inconsistent, neglectful, or emotionally distant caregiving, teaching us to depend on ourselves and keep our emotions protected. We start to link vulnerability with pain and develop defenses to shield ourselves from getting hurt again.

These defenses can show up in different ways, often subtle and hard to detect. We might emphasize independence and self-reliance, downplaying the need for emotional support.

We could find it difficult to express our emotions or notice that we distance ourselves as relationships grow closer.

We might even become overly focused on our partner's flaws or start arguments to create space.

These actions aren't meant to be harmful; they're just misguided efforts to protect a heart that's been hurt before. However, while these behaviors might provide short-term comfort, they often end up preventing us from forming the deep, meaningful connections we truly desire.

James was one of those clients who walked into my office with an air of confidence that bordered on invincibility. From the moment he sat down, I could tell he was someone who was used to controlling every aspect of his life. He was in his early thirties, impeccably dressed, and exuded success.

He told me he was a top executive at a tech company in San Francisco, living the kind of life most people would envy— wealthy, respected, and constantly surrounded by people who admired him. Yet, as we began to talk, it became clear that behind the polished exterior was a man deeply troubled by a gnawing sense of emptiness.

James didn't come to therapy because he felt broken or lost. In fact, he seemed almost reluctant to be there, as though admitting he needed help was a sign of weakness. But he couldn't shake the feeling that something was off.

He had everything he thought he wanted, but it all felt hollow. Relationships were particularly challenging for him. Despite his charm and good looks, he couldn't maintain a romantic relationship for more than a few months. Whenever things started to get serious, he found himself pulling away, unable to connect on a deeper level.

In our sessions, James rarely talked about his emotions. He described his life in terms of achievements—another promotion, another successful deal, another accolade. It was like he had a checklist of accomplishments, and emotions didn't make the cut. I asked him about his childhood, and he spoke about it as if it were just another chapter in his success story.

He was the eldest of three boys, raised by a father who was a self-made millionaire and a mother who was a perfectionist. Failure was not an option in their household, and any sign of vulnerability was seen as a flaw to be corrected.

One day, after several weeks of guarded conversations, James mentioned a recurring dream that had been bothering him. In the dream, he was in a grand, empty mansion, frantically trying to clean it.

No matter how much he scrubbed and dusted, the dirt kept piling up, spreading to every corner of the house. He described the dream with the same detachment he used for everything else, but I could sense there was more to it.

I asked him what he thought the mansion represented. At first, he dismissed the dream as meaningless, just a random creation of his mind. But as we talked, something seemed to click.

The mansion, he realized, was a symbol of his life—grand, impressive on the outside, but empty and overwhelming inside.

The dirt that kept accumulating was all the emotions and fears he had been sweeping under the rug for years. No matter how hard he tried to maintain the perfect image, the mess inside was getting harder to ignore.

The breakthrough came when James shared a memory he hadn't thought about in years. He was twelve years old, and his dog, Max, had just died. It was the first time he had experienced real loss. He remembered sitting in his room, crying quietly, when his father walked in. His father, a man who prided himself on his stoicism, looked at him with a mix of disappointment and impatience.

"Crying isn't going to bring him back, James. You need to toughen up," he had said. James wiped his tears, nodded, and from that moment on, he decided that showing emotion was a weakness he couldn't afford.

That memory was the key to understanding why James had built such high walls around himself.

He had spent his entire life trying to live up to an impossible standard of perfection, believing that if he could just keep everything under control, he would be safe from the pain of failure or rejection. But in doing so, he had also kept himself from experiencing real connection and intimacy.

THE ROOTS OF AVOIDANT ATTACHMENT

Our earliest experiences, much like seeds sown in the rich soil of our childhood, significantly influence how we connect with others throughout our lives.

Attachment theory, developed by British psychologist John Bowlby and later expanded by Mary Ainsworth, provides a captivating perspective on the complexities of human relationships.

It's akin to a behind-the-scenes view of a blockbuster film, except this movie is your life, and the leading roles are played by your relationships.

At its foundation, attachment theory posits that our primary caregivers, typically our parents, are pivotal in shaping our attachment style. It's not just about the warmth and affection we receive; it's about how consistently our needs for comfort, safety, and emotional support are met during our formative years.

Like a thermostat setting the temperature, these early interactions with caregivers establish the baseline for our emotional regulation and expectations in relationships.

Imagine learning to ride a bike. If your parents patiently supported you, holding the seat and encouraging you as you learned to balance, you likely developed a sense of trust and security.

You knew that even if you fell, they would be there to help you back up. This experience is similar to forming a secure attachment style, where you feel comfortable with intimacy, trust your partner, and can express your needs openly.

However, if your parents were overprotective, never letting go of the bike seat and constantly warning you of dangers, you might have grown up feeling smothered and overly dependent, leading to an anxious attachment style.

In this case, you might crave closeness but always fear being abandoned.

Now, consider if your parents were more like absent-minded professors who forgot they were supposed to be teaching you to ride. You might have felt neglected and unimportant, leading you to rely solely on yourself for emotional support. This scenario can contribute to developing an avoidant attachment style, where you prioritize independence and avoid emotional closeness as if it were something to be avoided at all costs.

Inconsistent, neglectful, or emotionally distant caregiving can feel like a rough, unpredictable bike ride, leaving you insecure and unsure of what to expect. When your emotional needs are not consistently met, you might learn to suppress them, thinking, "Why bother sharing my feelings if no one will respond?"

This can lead to avoidant attachment, where self-reliance and emotional distance become your defense mechanisms against potential pain.

These early experiences form what attachment theorists refer to as "internal working models" – mental blueprints that shape our understanding of relationships and intimacy.

These models are like the little voices in your head that tell you, "You're not good enough," or "You can't trust anyone." If your early experiences taught you that love is unreliable or that vulnerability leads to pain, your internal working model might be one of fear and avoidance.

But there's good news: these internal working models aren't permanent. Through self-awareness, understanding, and intentional effort, we can rewrite these blueprints and develop healthier patterns of relating. It's like upgrading from an old, outdated phone – the transition might take some time, but the new features and capabilities are worth it.

Understanding the roots of avoidant attachment is the first step toward healing and growth. By reflecting on our early experiences and recognizing how they've shaped our beliefs about relationships, we can begin to challenge those limiting beliefs and foster new, more secure ways of connecting with others.

The journey may not always be easy, but the rewards are immeasurable. As the saying goes, "The best time to plant a tree was 20 years ago. The second best time is now."

SIGNS OF AVOIDANT ATTACHMENT

- Fear of commitment and a preference for short-term relationships
- Minimizing or dismissing their own emotional needs
- Discomfort with vulnerability and expressing emotions
- Strong preference for self-reliance and independence
- Difficulty trusting others and relying on them for support
- Tendency to withdraw or become distant when emotional intimacy increases
- Difficulty maintaining long-term, committed relationships

E X E R C I S E

Create a timeline of significant early experiences and relationships. Identify any key events or relationships that might have influenced your attachment style. Reflect on how these experiences might have shaped your current patterns of behavior and emotional responses.

Objective: To map out significant early experiences and relationships, and understand their impact on current attachment behaviors and emotional responses.

Step-by-Step Instructions

Create a Timeline:

- Materials Needed: Paper, pen, or digital tool (e.g., a word processor or spreadsheet).
- Action: Draw a timeline from your earliest childhood years to the present. Mark key ages or periods (e.g., ages 0-5, 6-10, 11-15.).
- Focus Points: Include major life events such as family changes (e.g., divorce, relocation), significant relationships (e.g., with parents, siblings, caregivers), and any events that felt particularly impactful.

Identify Key Experiences:

Action: Under each marked period on your timeline, list significant experiences or relationships. This might include:

- Positive experiences (e.g., supportive relationships, achievements).
- Negative experiences (e.g., neglect, emotional unavailability, loss).
- Details: Write brief descriptions of these experiences and how they affected you at the time.

Use the template below for this effect or use it as a guide to create yours.

AGE 0-5

Significant life Events (e.g., divorce, relocation), significant relationships (e.g., with parents, siblings, caregivers)

For every life events, write out the emotions attached to it whether positive or negative emotion

AGE 0-5

Significant life Events (e.g., divorce, relocation), significant relationships (e.g., with parents, siblings, caregivers)

For every life events, write out the emotions attached to it whether positive or negative emotion

AGE 6-10

Significant life Events (e.g., divorce, relocation), significant relationships (e.g., with parents, siblings, caregivers)

For every life events, write out the emotions attached to it whether positive or negative emotion

AGE 6-10

Significant life Events (e.g., divorce, relocation), significant relationships (e.g., with parents, siblings, caregivers)

For every life events, write out the emotions attached to it whether positive or negative emotion

AGE 11-15

Significant life Events (e.g., divorce, relocation), significant relationships (e.g., with parents, siblings, caregivers)

For every life events, write out the emotions attached to it whether positive or negative emotion

AGE 11-15

Significant life Events (e.g., divorce, relocation), significant relationships (e.g., with parents, siblings, caregivers)

For every life events, write out the emotions attached to it whether positive or negative emotion

In what ways do I see avoidant behaviors or patterns showing up in my current or past relationships, such as difficulties with closeness or communication?

____

____

____

____

How does my avoidant attachment style affect my ability to form and maintain meaningful connections with others, and what impact does this have on my relationships?

____

____

____

____

"Love is not about possession. Love is about appreciation." — Osho

Chapter 2

THE FEAR OF CLOSENESS

When I first started my private practice in Seattle, I was eager to apply the theories I had learned during my training, particularly about avoidant attachment.

One of my early clients, Sam, seemed to fit the profile perfectly. He was a young professional who had come to therapy because he felt his relationships were always falling short. Despite our work together, Sam was consistently distant and often canceled appointments last minute.

One day, after a particularly difficult session, Sam suddenly became evasive. He was avoiding eye contact and seemed on edge.

It was unlike him, and I couldn't figure out why. After a few more missed sessions, I grew concerned and decided to check in. To my surprise, Sam admitted that he had been seeing another therapist without telling me.

It turned out that Sam had found another therapist through a recommendation from a friend. This new therapist used a highly unconventional method that conflicted with my approach.

The sessions involved intense, almost confrontational techniques that seemed to push Sam's boundaries in ways he wasn't ready for. Sam said he felt overwhelmed and confused, and it had exacerbated his avoidance rather than helping.

The twist came when Sam finally opened up about his deep-seated fears. The new therapist's approach had triggered an emotional floodgate, causing him to retreat even further. He realized that he had been trying to avoid dealing with his core issues by jumping between therapists and methods, thinking that one might be better than the other.

Sam's admission led to a critical conversation between us. I was able to address the specific ways the new therapy had intensified his avoidance and offered a more balanced approach that incorporated elements from both methods.

We worked together to create a customized plan that respected his pace and addressed his fears directly.
The real breakthrough occurred during a session where Sam's long-hidden fears about his relationships came to light. His experience with the new therapist had given him the insight to confront these fears, and he began to see patterns he hadn't recognized before.

He realized that his avoidant behaviors were not just a reaction to therapy but a fundamental part of how he dealt with intimacy and trust.

The fear of closeness isn't a conscious choice but a deeply ingrained response, often stemming from early childhood experiences. It's a paradox: a desire for connection coupled with an instinctive withdrawal from intimacy. This internal struggle can lead to perplexing behavior patterns in relationships, leaving both partners feeling frustrated and confused.

When we examine this fear more closely, we uncover a complex mix of emotions and beliefs. There's the fear of being overwhelmed—feeling smothered or losing independence in a relationship.

There's the dread of rejection—worrying about being abandoned or criticized for being ourselves. And there's the anxiety about vulnerability—feeling uneasy about opening up and risking potential hurt.

These fears are not baseless. They often arise from early experiences where emotional needs were unmet, boundaries were crossed, or vulnerability was met with criticism or neglect.

As children, we develop coping mechanisms to handle these painful situations. We learn to protect ourselves by creating emotional distance, suppressing our needs, and prioritizing self-reliance.

While these protective strategies help us as children, they can become obstacles to intimacy as we grow older and enter adult relationships.

We might unconsciously replicate childhood dynamics, pushing away those who get too close or withdrawing when vulnerability feels overwhelming.

The fear of closeness is a potent force, often operating below our conscious awareness. It can show up in subtle ways— hesitating to share personal thoughts or feelings, prioritizing work or hobbies over relationship time, or creating distance through arguments or criticism of a partner.

Acknowledging this fear is the first step toward healing and growth. It involves exploring our past, understanding the roots of our avoidant tendencies, and challenging the negative beliefs that prevent us from forming intimate connections. This journey requires self-discovery, compassion, and courage.

HOW AVOIDANTS PROTECT THEMSELVES FROM INTIMACY

The avoidant's range of deactivation strategies is surprisingly varied. Imagine this: your partner suddenly becomes overly critical, focusing on minor flaws like a heat-seeking missile. A missed chore, a slightly offhand comment, or even a harmless misunderstanding can spark a major argument.

It seems as if they're actively seeking reasons to create distance, preemptively defending against the vulnerability that comes with closeness.

Another common tactic in the Deactivation Dance is the emotional disappearing act. Just when things seem to be going well, your partner might retreat, becoming emotionally unavailable. Conversations turn superficial, affection diminishes, and shared activities lose their charm. It's like trying to embrace a cactus – you might get close, but it's going to hurt. This withdrawal can be deeply frustrating for the other partner, who is left confused about what went wrong.

Sometimes, the avoidant's deactivation strategies are less obvious but equally effective. They might immerse themselves in work or hobbies, using them as a barrier against emotional closeness.

While having interests is healthy, if these consistently take precedence over connecting with loved ones, it's a red flag. It's as if your partner is constructing a wall around their heart, one brick at a time, with every late night at the office or weekend spent on their latest project.

The avoidant's tendency to prioritize independence can also create distance. They might resist making joint decisions, sharing their emotions, or relying on their partner for support.

This strong desire for independence can be admirable in some situations, but in a relationship, it can lead to feelings of isolation and emotional disconnect. It's as if your partner is saying, "I care about you, but please don't get too close."

So, why do avoidants engage in this complex dance of distancing?

At its heart, it's a defense mechanism, a way to shield themselves from the perceived risks of intimacy. They might fear being hurt, rejected, or overwhelmed by their partner's emotions. They may have past traumas that make them cautious about getting too close or simply lack the skills to handle emotional intimacy healthily.

Regardless of the reasons, it's crucial to remember that these deactivation strategies are often unconscious. Avoidants aren't intentionally trying to harm their partners; they're merely trying to protect themselves. However, while these behaviors may provide temporary relief from anxiety or discomfort, they ultimately undermine the very thing they desire – a deep, meaningful connection.

The avoidant's distancing actions provoke feelings of hurt and insecurity in their partner, who might react with anger, clinginess, or their own withdrawal. This reinforces the avoidant's belief that intimacy is dangerous, leading to further distancing. It's a cycle that can persist for years, leaving both partners feeling lonely, frustrated, and unfulfilled.

E X E R C I S E

Create a "fear ladder" where you list your fears related to intimacy and closeness, starting with the smallest fear and working up to the biggest. This exercise can help you identify and confront your deepest concerns.

Objective: To identify and confront your fears about intimacy by ranking them from least to most intimidating.

Steps:

Gather Materials:

- What You Need: A piece of paper or a digital note, and a pen or typing tool.

Brainstorm Your Fears:

- Action: Start by listing all the fears or concerns you have about intimacy and closeness. Think about situations or feelings that make you uncomfortable or anxious.
- Examples: Fear of being vulnerable, fear of rejection, fear of losing independence.

Rank Your Fears:

- Action: Place each fear you listed on the ladder, starting with the smallest fear on the lowest rung and working up to the biggest fear on the top rung.

Use the template below for this effect or use it as a guide to create yours.

FEARS

FEARS

____

____

____

____

____

____

____

____

____

____

How do I typically respond when I feel overwhelmed or threatened in a relationship?

____

____

____

____

What are the potential consequences of not addressing my fear of closeness?

____

____

____

____

"*The walls we build around us to keep sadness out also keep out the joy.*" — *Jim Rohn*

Chapter 3
DECODING DEACTIVATION SIGNALS

I first met Emily at Roosevelt Academy, a prestigious private school nestled in the heart of San Francisco. The school was known for its rigorous academics and well-rounded student body, but Emily stood out— not for her achievements, but for her silence.

She was one of those students who never made a fuss, always slipping into class quietly, sitting at the back, and rarely raising her hand. Her grades were impeccable, yet there was something unsettling about how she seemed to drift through the halls, almost like a ghost.

One day, I was reviewing student files when I noticed Emily's name. Straight A's in every subject, but not a single note about extracurricular activities, not a single teacher's comment that gave any insight into who she really was.

Curious, I reached out to Mrs. Thompson, her English teacher, to get a better sense of Emily. Mrs. Thompson was warm and approachable, the kind of teacher students usually flocked to, but even she admitted that Emily was a mystery.

"She's brilliant, no doubt about it," Mrs. Thompson told me over coffee in the teacher's lounge. "But she never participates. It's like she's here but not really present, you know?"

That stuck with me. I decided to meet with Emily, inviting her to my office under the guise of discussing her college plans. She arrived promptly, her face a mask of politeness, but I could sense the wall she'd put up.

We talked about her classes, her plans for the future, but she offered little more than surface-level responses. There was no spark, no sign of what made her tick.

Over the next few weeks, I made it a point to check in with Emily periodically, always casually, never pushing too hard.

I could see her start to relax around me, but the emotional distance remained. It wasn't until Mrs. Thompson assigned a creative writing project that things began to change.

The assignment was simple: write an essay about something meaningful in your life. It was an open-ended prompt, designed to let students explore their thoughts and feelings freely.

When I asked Emily about the assignment, she shrugged it off, saying she hadn't decided on a topic yet. But I could see something flicker in her eyes—a hesitation, a hint of vulnerability. I let it go, hoping she'd find her way to express herself.

A few days later, I was in the library, searching for a book, when I spotted Emily sitting alone at a table, her head bent over a notebook.

She was so absorbed in her writing that she didn't notice me standing nearby. I didn't want to intrude, so I left her to her thoughts, but I couldn't shake the image of her intense focus.

A week passed, and I didn't hear anything more about the essay. Then, one afternoon, Daniel, a bright and outspoken student who was the closest thing Emily had to a friend, came to see me. He seemed agitated, nervously twisting a piece of paper in his hands.

"I found this," he said, handing me what looked like a torn-out page from a notebook. "It's Emily's. She left it behind in the library. I think you should read it."

I unfolded the paper, my eyes scanning the neat handwriting. It was an essay—raw, powerful, and heartbreakingly honest. Emily had written about her father, who had been battling severe depression for years.

She described how his illness had consumed their family, how she had learned to fend for herself emotionally, withdrawing from everyone around her. She wrote about the fear that had haunted her for so long—the fear that if she let anyone in, they would see the cracks, the fragility she hid beneath her perfect grades and quiet demeanor.

I felt a pang in my chest as I read her words. This was the real Emily, the girl she'd been hiding from the world. But what struck me the most was the last line of the essay: "I don't want to be invisible anymore."

Avoidant attachment isn't a lack of wanting intimacy; it's rooted in a deep-seated fear of it. This creates a paradox where the desire for closeness exists alongside a strong instinct to keep distance. This inner conflict often shows up in subtle ways through what are known as "deactivation signals."

Deactivation signals act like warning lights in a relationship. They are the small, often unnoticed cues—both verbal and nonverbal—that an avoidantly attached person gives off when they feel threatened by closeness or vulnerability. These signals can be as subtle as a change in voice tone or body language, or they can be more obvious, like starting an argument or emotionally pulling away.

Research published in the Journal of Personality and Social Psychology found that people with avoidant attachment are more likely to show deactivation signals when their partner seeks closeness. These signals could include turning away, folding their arms, or changing the subject.

The problem with deactivation signals is that they are often so subtle they go unnoticed or are misinterpreted. This can leave partners feeling confused, frustrated, and uncertain about where they stand.

Recognizing these signals is vital for both the avoidant person and their partner. For the avoidantly attached, becoming aware of their own deactivation habits is a key step toward breaking the cycle of emotional distance. It helps them see how they unconsciously undermine intimacy and connection.

For the partner, understanding these deactivation signals offers insight into their loved one's behavior. It enables them to respond with compassion and understanding rather than reacting with hurt or anger. It also helps them set healthy boundaries and communicate their needs more effectively.

EMOTIONAL VS. PHYSICAL DISTANCE

In relationships, it's easy to confuse being physically close with being emotionally connected. You can sit right next to your partner, yet feel distant in a way that physical proximity can't bridge. This is especially common in people with avoidant attachment.

For those with avoidant attachment, being physically present is straightforward. They can go on dinner dates, cuddle during movies, and even say "I love you" with genuine intent. However, the real challenge lies beneath the surface.

Emotional intimacy, which truly holds relationships together, involves being vulnerable, trusting, and open about your deepest thoughts and feelings.

For someone with avoidant attachment, this level of closeness feels like walking on broken glass. They instinctively keep an emotional distance to protect themselves from potential hurt.

This doesn't mean they don't care; rather, expressing and receiving love on a deep emotional level feels risky. It's as if they have a locked vault inside where their true feelings are hidden, but they no longer know how to open it. They may desire connection, but their fear of intimacy stops them from fully opening up.

The impact of this emotional disconnect can be significant. Initially, a partner might be drawn to the avoidant's independent and self-sufficient demeanor, but over time, the lack of emotional depth can take a toll. It's like trying to drink from a mirage—it looks promising but leaves you unfulfilled.

Partners of avoidant individuals often end up feeling confused, frustrated, and even unloved.

They might go out of their way to close the gap—by showering the avoidant with affection, initiating deep conversations, or offering constant reassurance.

However, their efforts often meet resistance, leaving them feeling rejected and emotionally exhausted.

It's similar to the scene in "The Notebook" where Noah writes Allie a letter every day for a year, but she never receives them. The love is there, but it's blocked. For those with avoidant attachment, that blockage is the fear of intimacy.

EXERCISE

Keep a journal for a week, noting any instances where you or your partner exhibit deactivation signals. Reflect on the patterns and triggers that contribute to these behaviors.

Step-by-Step Instructions

Prepare Your Journal:

- Materials Needed: A notebook, journal, or a digital device where you can write daily entries.
- Setup: Create a dedicated section in your journal titled "Deactivation Signals Journal." You might want to set aside a specific time each day to write your entries.

Understand Deactivation Signals:

- Definition: Deactivation signals are behaviors that you or your partner might use to create emotional distance or to avoid closeness in a relationship. Examples include withdrawing from conversations, avoiding physical touch, becoming overly critical, or focusing excessively on work or hobbies.

- Examples: Write down a few common deactivation signals that you think you or your partner might use. This will help you identify them more easily during the week.

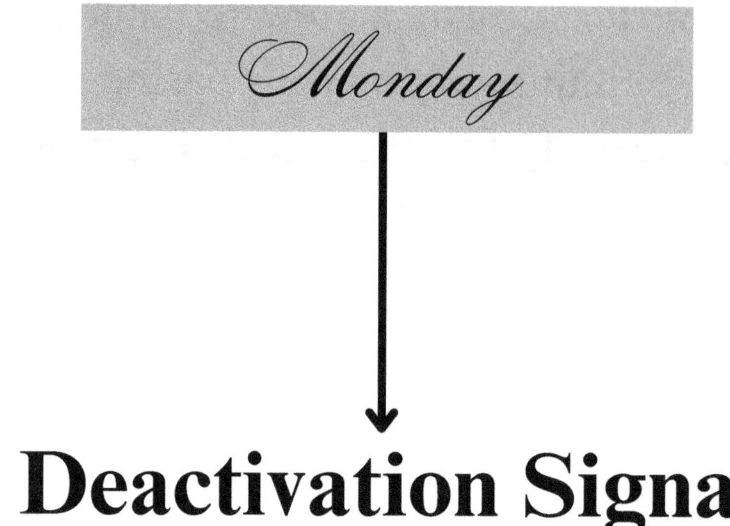

Deactivation Signal

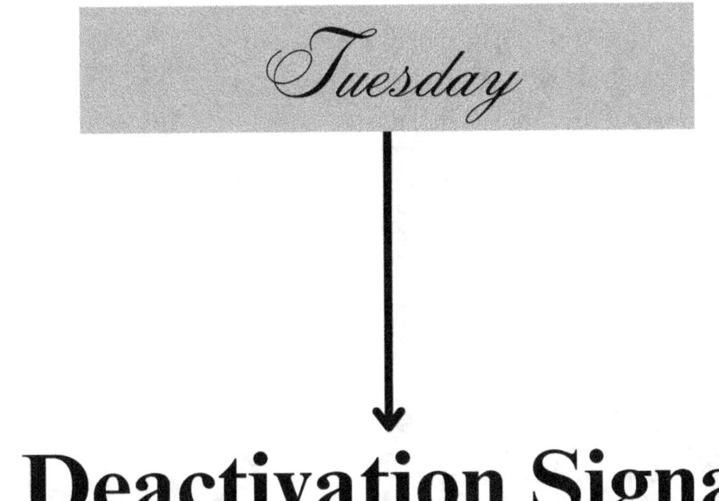

Deactivation Signal

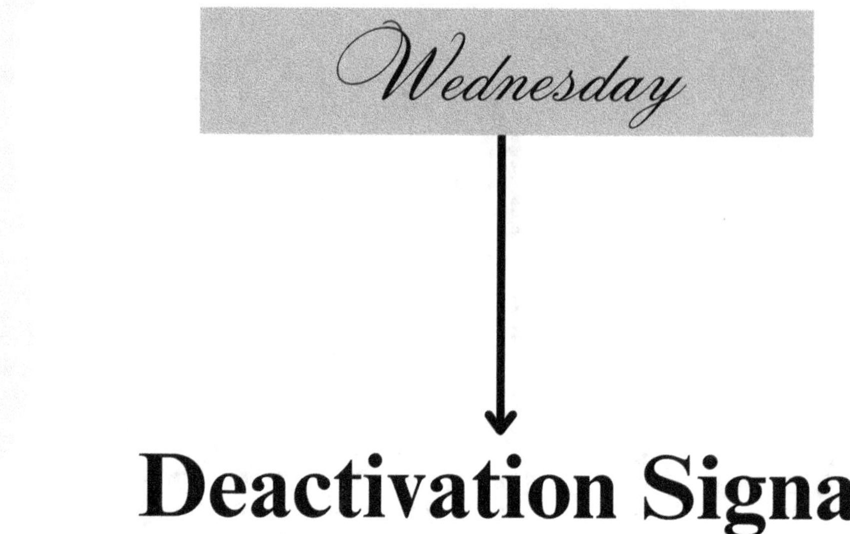

Deactivation Signal

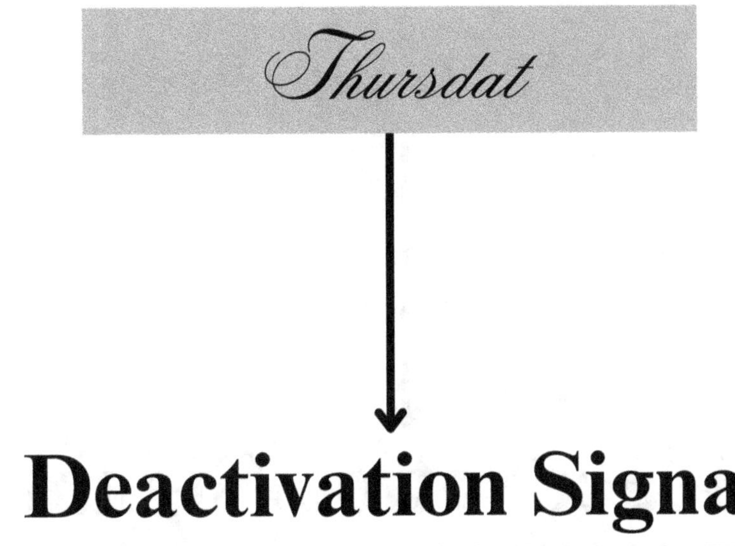

Deactivation Signal

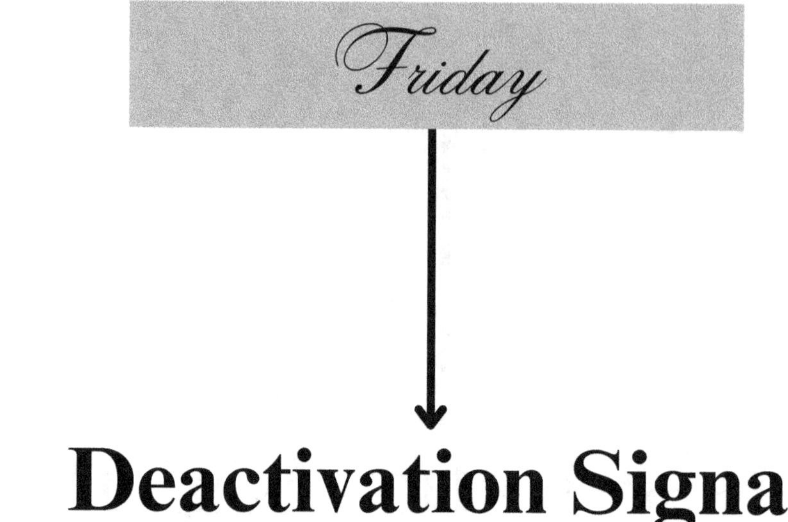

Deactivation Signal

Deactivation Signal

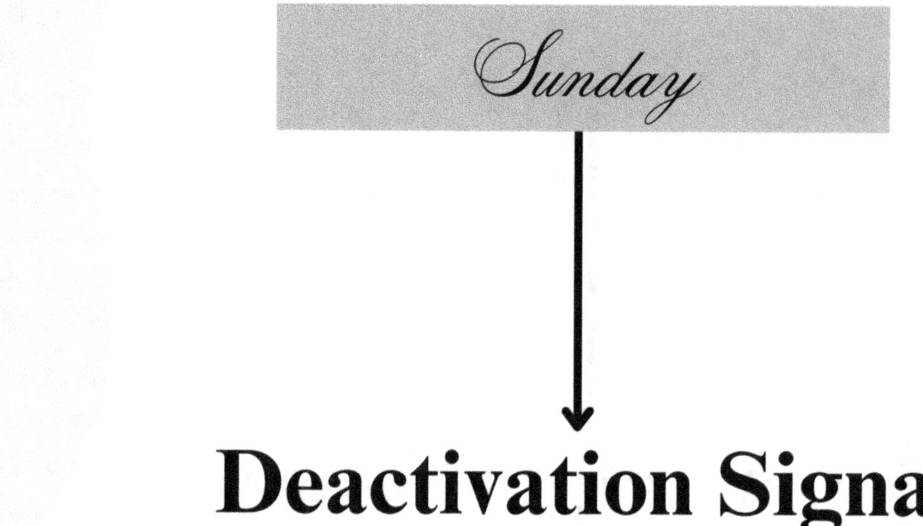

Deactivation Signal

What are my most common deactivation signals? How do they manifest in my relationships?

____

____

____

____

What are some healthier ways I can communicate my need for space or distance without shutting down completely?

____

____

____

____

"*The way we talk to our children becomes their inner voice.*" — *Peggy O'Mara*

Chapter 4
THE PATH TO SECURE ATTACHMENT

When Lily came to live with her adoptive parents, Sylvia and Donald, everything seemed to be falling into place. They were thrilled to provide a stable and loving home for her, and Lily, who was just three years old, seemed to be adjusting well at first.

Her new room was decorated with bright colors, and her parents made sure to spend quality time with her each day, reading books and playing games.

However, a few months into the adoption, things began to take a troubling turn. Lily, who had initially been warm and affectionate, started to exhibit extreme emotional outbursts and anxiety. She would suddenly cry inconsolably or lash out over seemingly minor issues.

Her behavior was unpredictable, and Sylvia and Donald felt helpless as they tried to navigate these new challenges.

One rainy afternoon, while Sylvia was sorting through some old family photos for a scrapbook project, Lily came across an old photo album in the attic.

The album was filled with pictures of her from her earlier foster placements. I remember vividly when Sylvia called me in distress, saying that Lily had become deeply upset after finding the album. They had noticed that Lily's behavior worsened significantly following that incident.

I decided to visit Sylvia and Donald to help them understand what might be going on. As we sat down to talk, Sylvia showed me the photo album.

The images depicted various foster homes and caregivers, and there was one particular photo that caught my eye—a picture of Lily with an older woman who seemed to be her caregiver during one of her placements.

There was something unsettling about the way Lily reacted to that photo, almost as if it triggered a deep, buried pain.

We began to explore Lily's early life more thoroughly, and I learned that her previous placements had been marked by instability and trauma. Lily had experienced multiple foster homes, each with different caregivers, and the disruptions had left emotional scars.

This history of upheaval and inconsistency had left her feeling deeply unsettled and triggered by reminders of her past.

In therapy sessions with Lily, we used play therapy techniques to help her express her emotions and process her experiences.

I worked closely with Sylvia and Donald, guiding them on how to provide a stable, predictable environment for Lily. We implemented routines that gave Lily a sense of security, like consistent mealtimes and bedtime rituals.

The turning point came when we discovered that Lily had been experiencing sensory triggers related to her past trauma. For instance, certain smells and sounds from her previous foster homes would set off her anxiety.

We used sensory integration techniques to help her cope with these triggers, and Sylvia and Donald became more attuned to Lily's needs.

HEALING THE WOUNDS

The path to secure attachment can be a bumpy ride, especially if your childhood resembled something out of "The Addams Family" rather than "Leave It to Beaver."

If your early relationships with caregivers weren't ideal, you probably have some emotional baggage to sort through. Think of this chapter as your personal emotional yard sale, where you get to declutter and make sense of what's been weighing you down.

Avoiding these old wounds is like trying to build a gingerbread house on a wobbly foundation—it's bound to collapse. Those unresolved childhood issues can spill over into your adult relationships, leading to patterns of emotional distance and a fear of closeness.

Facing these past hurts isn't about wallowing in negativity. It's about understanding how those early experiences shaped your self-view and your approach to relationships.

It's about recognizing the defense mechanisms you developed—those emotional walls you built to keep yourself safe. While these strategies might have protected you as a child, they can hinder your ability to form healthy connections as an adult.

You might wonder, "Isn't therapy just for people with major problems?" Think of it as a tune-up for your emotional engine. Just like you wouldn't drive a car with a sputtering engine, you shouldn't navigate relationships with faulty emotional wiring.

Various types of therapy can be beneficial for those with avoidant attachment. Attachment-focused therapy, for instance, helps you understand your attachment style and find healthier ways to relate. EMDR (Eye Movement Desensitization and Reprocessing) can be useful for processing traumatic memories, while somatic experiencing helps you connect with your body's sensations to release stored emotions.

But therapy isn't the only tool for healing. Self-reflection is key to understanding how your past influences your present.

Journaling provides a safe space to explore your thoughts, feelings, and behaviors without judgment—like your personal "Dear Diary" session where you can be completely honest with yourself.

Inner child work is another powerful method. That scared, lonely, or unloved little kid inside you is still there and needs attention. Picture yourself comforting and reassuring your younger self, offering the love they didn't get.

This can be done through visualizations, writing letters to your inner child, or simply talking to them in your mind. It might seem a bit unconventional, but it can be incredibly effective.

BUILDING A
SECURE BASE

A solid and fulfilling relationship, particularly for those dealing with avoidant tendencies, relies on establishing a secure base.

This isn't about constructing a literal fort in your living room (though that might be fun), but rather creating an environment where both partners feel safe, understood, and emotionally supported.

Imagine your favorite coffee shop in downtown Los Angeles—the one with the cozy, worn leather couches, the perfect playlist, and a barista who remembers your regular order. That's your secure base: a place where you can unwind, be yourself, and recharge without fearing judgment or rejection.

The first key ingredient is emotional attunement. This involves being fully present with your partner, tuning into their verbal and nonverbal cues, and responding in a way that acknowledges their feelings.

It's not about solving their problems or giving unsolicited advice, but about letting them know, "I hear you, I see you, and I'm here for you."

Next is responsiveness. This means being available for your partner when they need you, both physically and emotionally. It involves responding to their texts, attending their important events, and offering a listening ear during tough times. For those with avoidant tendencies, actions often speak louder than words.

Lastly, consistent support is crucial. This means being there for your partner day after day, even when it's inconvenient or challenging. It's about celebrating their victories, comforting them during setbacks, and reminding them of their worth, even when they struggle to see it themselves. Think of it as being their personal cheerleader, but with fewer pom-poms and more meaningful conversations.

EXERCISE

Secure Base Visualization Exercise

Objective: To create a mental image of a safe and supportive space that fosters feelings of security, which can help in developing a more secure attachment style.

Step-by-Step Instructions

Find a Quiet Space:

- Action: Choose a comfortable and quiet place where you won't be disturbed. This could be a cozy chair, your bed, or a peaceful spot in your home.
- Environment: Ensure the space is free from distractions and allows you to relax completely.

Get Comfortable:

- **Action:** Sit or lie down in a comfortable position. Allow your body to relax and let go of any tension.
- **Breathing:** Take a few deep breaths to calm your mind and body. Inhale slowly through your nose, hold for a moment, and then exhale gently through your mouth.

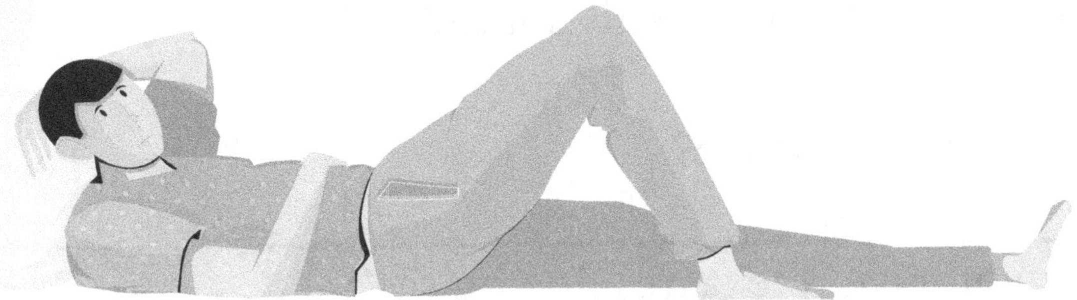

Close Your Eyes:

- **Action:** Gently close your eyes to help focus inward and block out external stimuli.
- **Relaxation:** Continue to take slow, deep breaths as you prepare to enter the visualization.

Visualize Your Secure Base:

- Action: Imagine a space where you feel completely safe, loved, and accepted. This could be a real place from your past, a fictional environment, or a blend of different elements that evoke a sense of security.

Envision the details of this space—

what does it look like?

____

What colors and textures do you see?

____

Is there a specific temperature or ambiance?

____

Notice any sounds, smells, or sensations that contribute to the feeling of safety.

Immerse Yourself in the Visualization:

- Action: Spend a few minutes fully immersing yourself in this mental image. Imagine yourself in this space, feeling supported and cared for.
- Physical Sensations: Pay attention to how this visualization makes you feel in your body. Notice any changes in your physical sensations or emotions as you engage with this secure space.

Reflect on Your Feelings:

- Action: After spending a few minutes in the visualization, gently bring your focus back to the present moment. Take a few more deep breaths to ground yourself.
- Reflection: Reflect on the feelings and sensations you experienced. How did the visualization affect your sense of security and well-being?

Reflect on Your Feelings:

- Action: After spending a few minutes in the visualization, gently bring your focus back to the present moment. Take a few more deep breaths to ground yourself.
- Reflection: Reflect on the feelings and sensations you experienced. How did the visualization affect your sense of security and well-being?

Incorporate into Daily Routine:

- Action: Consider incorporating this visualization exercise into your daily routine, especially during moments of stress or when you need to reconnect with feelings of safety and support.
- Frequency: Practice this exercise regularly to strengthen your sense of security and to help build a more secure attachment style.

This exercise helps you create a mental refuge that fosters feelings of safety and unconditional support, which can be a valuable tool for developing a more secure attachment style and managing stress or insecurity.

What qualities do I need in a partner or support system to feel safe and secure?

____

____

____

____

____

What are some small, actionable steps I can take today to move towards developing secure attachment?

____

____

____

____

____

Chapter 5

COMMUNICATION FOR CONNECTION

few years ago, I was working with a mother and daughter who seemed to be living in completely different worlds, even though they shared the same house. The mother was a successful attorney, always busy, always on the go, and very proud of the life she had built.

Her daughter, on the other hand, was a quiet, artistic teenager who spent most of her time in her room, painting or writing in her journal.

They hardly spoke beyond the basic exchanges necessary to get through the day. The mother often complained to me that her daughter was distant, unmotivated, and didn't seem to care about anything other than her art.

Meanwhile, the daughter felt like her mother only saw her as a project to be fixed, someone who needed to be more outgoing, more ambitious, more like the mother herself.

One day, while tidying up her daughter's room, the mother stumbled upon a small, leather-bound journal hidden under a pile of clothes. Curiosity got the better of her, and she opened it.

The first few entries were innocent enough—typical teenage musings about school and friends. But as she read on, the tone shifted. The entries became darker, filled with pain and loneliness.

The daughter wrote about feeling like she was never enough for her mother, like nothing she did could ever make her proud. There was a particularly heart-wrenching entry where the daughter confessed that she had thought about running away, just to see if her mother would even notice she was gone.

The mother's heart sank as she read these words. She had no idea her daughter felt this way. It was like a punch to the gut, realizing that the person she loved most in the world had been suffering in silence, right under her nose.

But instead of confronting her daughter immediately, she decided to take a different approach.

She left the journal open on her daughter's bed, with a simple note beside it: "I'm sorry. I'm ready to listen whenever you're ready to talk."

When her daughter came home and found the note, she was furious. She felt violated, betrayed that her mother had read something so personal without her permission. She stormed into the living room, journal in hand, and demanded to know why her mother had invaded her privacy.

The mother, for the first time in a long time, didn't react defensively. She just sat there, tears in her eyes, and apologized.

She explained that she had been so caught up in her own world that she hadn't noticed how far apart they had drifted. She admitted that she didn't know how to be the mother her daughter needed but was willing to learn if her daughter would help her.

The daughter didn't forgive her mother right away. It took time—weeks, in fact. But slowly, they began to rebuild their relationship. The mother suggested that they have weekly tea talks, just the two of them, where the daughter could share whatever was on her mind without fear of judgment.

At first, these talks were awkward and strained, but as the weeks passed, they started to look forward to them. The daughter began to open up about her feelings, and the mother learned to listen without trying to fix everything.

One of the key challenges in communication for those with avoidant attachment is learning to clearly and directly express their needs. This can feel intimidating, as the fear of vulnerability often leads to indirect communication, passive-aggressive behavior, or even complete withdrawal.

Yet, by taking the bold step of openly stating their needs, individuals with avoidant attachment can foster a deeper understanding with their partners and create opportunities for mutual support.

Of course, communication isn't always straightforward, even with the best intentions. Conflicts are a natural part of any relationship, and for those with avoidant attachment, these conflicts can stir up deep fears of rejection and abandonment.

However, by approaching disagreements with a desire to understand rather than a need to win, individuals and couples can learn to navigate conflicts constructively, ultimately strengthening their bond.

EXPRESSING
YOUR NEEDS

"Honey, I'm home!" Your partner calls out, kicking off their shoes by the door. Your heart skips a beat—not from excitement, but from a familiar pang of anxiety. It's a feeling you know well, a silent alarm signaling an impending wave of discomfort as the distance between the two of you closes.

Dinner conversation is pleasant enough, but it's all surface-level: sports scores, work anecdotes, the latest Netflix binge. Underneath the pleasantries, your emotional needs simmer like a pot threatening to boil over.

If this scenario resonates with you, it's likely that you have a touch of the "avoidant attachment" style.

It's like being wired to crave connection but then slamming on the brakes when things get too close. You want love, but vulnerability terrifies you.

So, how do you break this pattern? How do you voice what you need without the fear of being swallowed whole or pushed away?

Recognizing Needs: The First Step

The journey starts with recognizing that expressing your needs isn't a weakness; it's a superpower. Just like Superman needs his sunlight, you need emotional nourishment. And just like Superman doesn't always have it easy saving the world, expressing your needs can be challenging, especially if you've been conditioned to believe it's "needy" or "clingy."

First things first: identify what you need. This isn't always easy, especially if you've spent years building walls around your heart.

Think of it like a car dashboard. When the "low fuel" light comes on, you don't ignore it, right? You fill up the tank. Emotional needs are similar—they signal what's missing in your emotional tank.

Are you feeling unheard? Unappreciated? Lonely even when you're in the same room as your partner? Recognizing these signals is the first step toward filling your tank back up.

Finding Your Voice

Next, comes the challenge of finding your voice. Avoidant attachment often comes with a side of "I'm fine" syndrome. We bury our feelings like a squirrel hoarding nuts for winter.

But remember, expressing your needs isn't complaining; it's communicating. Instead of saying, "You never listen to me," try, "I feel unheard when I share my day, and I'd love for you to just listen sometimes."

Here's a pro tip: start small. Don't unload your entire emotional baggage on your partner all at once. Begin with expressing a simple need. Maybe it's, "I need a hug," or "I'd appreciate it if you checked in with me during the day."

Using "I" Statements: A Game-Changer

Using "I" statements can be a game-changer. It shifts the focus from blaming your partner to owning your feelings. Saying "I feel hurt when..." is much more constructive than saying, "You always make me feel..."

Boundaries: Your Emotional Fence

Think of boundaries as your emotional fence—they protect your space and allow you to control what comes in and out. Setting boundaries is crucial for anyone, but especially for those with avoidant attachment.

For example, if you need some alone time to recharge, communicate that to your partner. Don't ghost them or make excuses. Simply say, "I love spending time with you, but I also need some time to myself to recharge. I'll be back in an hour."

Rejection and Judgment: The Avoidant's Kryptonite

One of the biggest hurdles for people with avoidant attachment is the fear of rejection or judgment.
You worry that if you express your needs, your partner will see you as weak, needy, or demanding.

This fear is understandable, but it's often based on past experiences or negative self-beliefs. The truth is, most people appreciate honesty and vulnerability. It creates a deeper connection and allows for greater intimacy.

If the fear is overwhelming, consider talking to a therapist. They can help you explore the root of your fears and develop coping strategies.

Expressing your needs doesn't make you weak; it makes you human. And in the end, it's the key to building the deep, meaningful connections that everyone—yes, even those with avoidant attachment—truly desires.

ACTIVE
LISTENING

Active listening is about being fully present with your partner, both emotionally and mentally. This means putting away distractions like your phone and giving your full attention to what they're saying. Instead of jumping in with solutions or advice, focus on truly understanding their feelings.

A simple way to do this is by reflecting back what you've heard, like saying, "It sounds like you're feeling really overwhelmed by work." This shows that you're engaged and helps your partner feel understood.

It's important to validate their emotions, even if you don't agree with everything they're saying. Acknowledging their feelings, like saying, "I can see why you're upset.

That sounds really frustrating," helps create a sense of connection. Avoid judging their thoughts or feelings; instead, approach them with curiosity and an open mind.

Creating a safe space for your partner to share their thoughts and feelings without fear of criticism or rejection is key.

This means being patient, supportive, and letting them know that you're there for them, no matter what.

Active listening is a skill that gets easier with practice. Start with small conversations and gradually build your confidence. Over time, you'll find that this approach helps strengthen your relationships and creates a deeper connection with those you care about.

E X E R C I S E

Create a list of your emotional needs in relationships (e.g., affection, validation, support, space). Then, write down how you typically express these needs, both verbally and non-verbally. Identify any areas where your communication could be clearer or more direct.

Step-by-Step Instructions

Prepare Your Materials:

- Materials Needed: Paper and pen, or a digital device for note-taking.
- Environment: Find a quiet and comfortable place where you can reflect without interruptions.

Identify Your Emotional Needs:

- Action: Start by creating a list of your emotional needs in relationships. These are the things you require to feel secure, valued, and connected.
- Examples of Emotional Needs:
    - Affection: Feeling loved and cared for.
    - Validation: Having your feelings and opinions acknowledged.

Personalize: Reflect on your own experiences and relationships. What do you need most from others to feel emotionally fulfilled?

Reflect on How You Express These Needs:
- Action: Next, write down how you usually communicate each of these needs to others. Think about both your verbal and non-verbal communication.
- Verbal Communication: How do you ask for what you need? Do you use clear and direct language, or do you hint at what you want?
- Non-Verbal Communication: How do you express your needs through body language, facial expressions, or actions? For example, do you withdraw when you need space, or do you give subtle cues when you need affection?

Examples:
- When I need support, I might say, "I'm feeling overwhelmed" (verbal).
- When I need affection, I might lean in closer or touch my partner's arm (non-verbal).

Identify Areas for Improvement:

- Action: Review your list and reflect on how effective your communication has been in getting your needs met. Identify any areas where your communication might be unclear, indirect, or misunderstood.
- Questions to Consider:
  - Are there times when I don't express my needs at all?
  - Do I rely on others to "guess" what I need rather than asking directly?
  - Are there specific needs that I find difficult to communicate?

To complete this exercise use the template below as a guide to create yours or use the one below.

My Emotional Needs

How I express Them

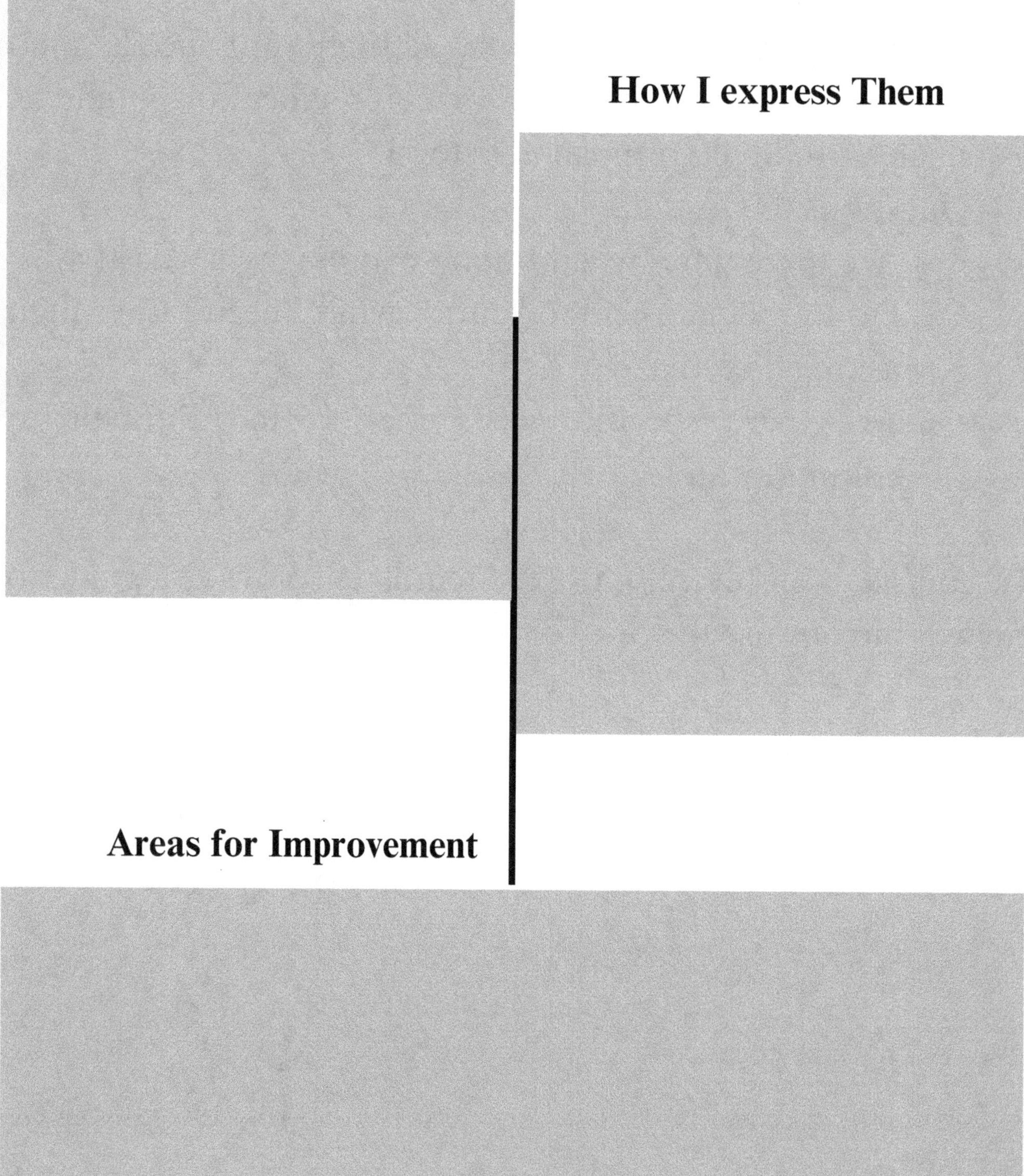

Areas for Improvement

My Emotional Needs

How I express Them

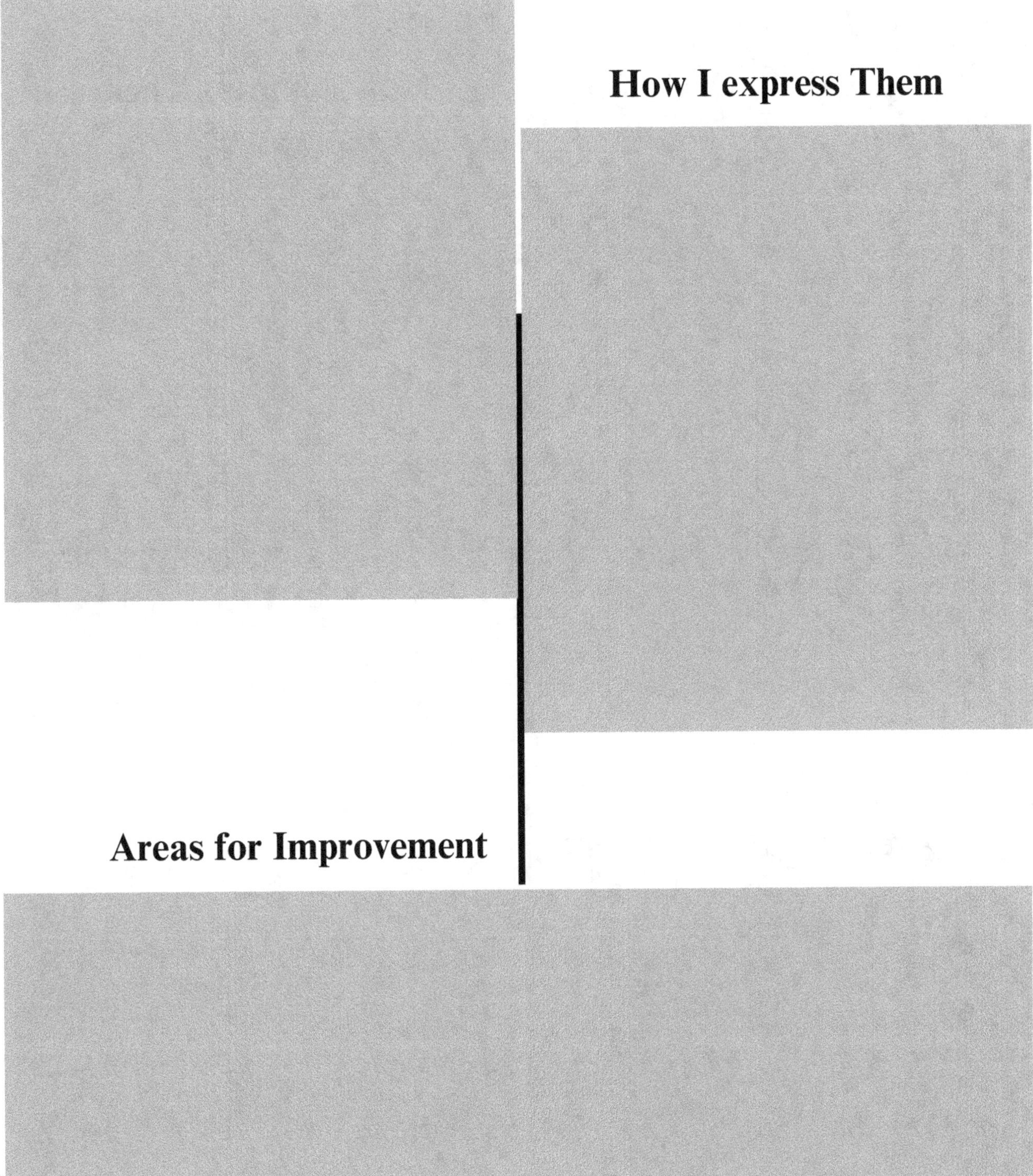

Areas for Improvement

My Emotional Needs

How I express Them

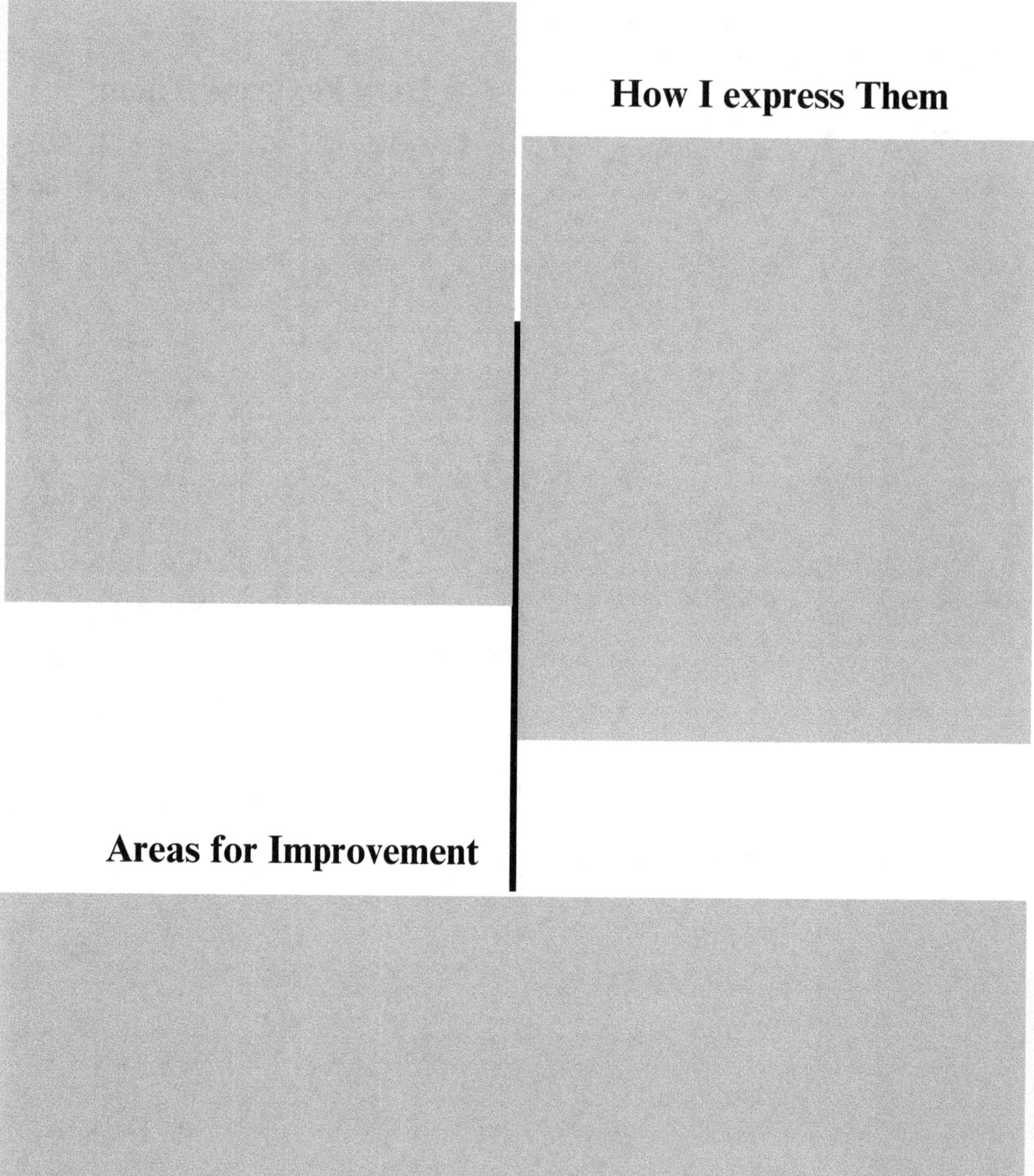

Areas for Improvement

What emotions do I find most difficult to express in my relationships? Why might that be?

____

____

____

____

What are some new communication strategies I can try to improve the way I express my needs and listen to my partner's?

____

____

____

____

"**The best thing to hold onto in life is each other.**" — **Audrey Hepburn**

Chapter 6

SELF-CARE FOR AVOIDANTS

A close friend of mine had always been the reliable one, the person everyone leaned on whenever they needed something. She was the type who would drop everything, no matter how inconvenient, to help a friend in need.

Over the years, I watched as she took on more and more—family obligations, work pressures, and endless favors for friends. It seemed like she had an endless well of energy, but I started noticing little cracks in her façade.

She would often cancel our plans last minute, citing exhaustion, and there were times when she seemed distant, lost in thought.

One summer, she surprised us all by deciding to take a solo trip to a remote cabin in the mountains.

This was entirely out of character for her;

she was someone who thrived on being around others and rarely did anything alone. When I asked her about the trip, she brushed it off, saying she needed some "me time" and that it was just a short getaway. But something in her voice told me there was more to it.

She left without much fanfare, and for the first week, we didn't hear much from her. A few texts here and there, nothing unusual. Then, the silence stretched on. I tried calling, texting—nothing. Days turned into weeks, and my worry grew. I even considered driving up to the cabin myself, but it was in such a remote area that I had no idea how to find it.

Finally, after what felt like forever, she called me. Her voice was different—calmer, more at peace. She told me she had spent those weeks disconnected from everything—no phone, no internet, just her and nature.

She had needed to get away, she said, to escape the constant demands of everyone around her. She confessed that she had been feeling overwhelmed for years, like she was drowning in other people's problems and expectations.

The pressure had been building, and she realized she had lost herself somewhere along the way.

While she was up there, she found an old sketchbook buried in one of the cabin's closets. As a child, she used to love drawing, but life had gotten in the way, and she had pushed that passion aside.

With nothing but time on her hands, she began sketching again, and it was like rediscovering a part of herself she had forgotten.

She spent hours drawing the landscape around her, the trees, the mountains, the animals that wandered near the cabin. Each stroke of the pencil felt like a release, a way to express everything she had been holding inside for so long.

When she finally came back, she was different. The friend who had always been there for everyone else had finally learned to be there for herself. She told me she had decided to make some changes in her life. She was going to set boundaries, say no when she needed to, and start putting her own needs first.

For those with avoidant attachment, self-care might seem contradictory. While the instinct is often to withdraw and isolate, self-care isn't about pulling away from others—it's about building a healthy relationship with yourself. It's about taking care of your emotional needs so you have the energy to connect meaningfully with others.

Think of self-care as refueling a car. If your car's tank is empty, it doesn't matter how much you want to keep driving—you won't get very far. Similarly, if you ignore your own needs, you'll run out of emotional energy, making it tough to be there for others or even for yourself. Self-care is how you fill up that tank, giving yourself the resilience to handle the ups and downs of relationships and life.

For people with avoidant tendencies, self-care can be a key to healing. When you prioritize your well-being, you're challenging the belief that your needs aren't important or that you have to rely only on yourself. Instead, you create a safe space within where you can explore your feelings, face your fears, and practice self-compassion.

HEALING EMOTIONAL NEGLECT

Let's go back to a part of you that's been quietly waiting for attention: your inner child. This isn't about New Age ideas or talking to stuffed animals. It's about reconnecting with the most genuine, vulnerable part of yourself—the part that holds the key to healing from avoidant attachment.

Imagine your inner child as the curious kid you once were, full of wonder and ready to explore the world. This child felt joy, sadness, fear, and anger—everything that makes us human. But somewhere along the way, maybe because of neglect, criticism, or unmet needs, this inner child got pushed aside, silenced, or even forgotten.

This isn't about blaming your parents or digging up old wounds. It's about recognizing that those early experiences shaped how you deal with emotions today, which might contribute to your avoidant tendencies. Maybe you learned to suppress your feelings to avoid being overwhelmed or rejected, or perhaps you built emotional walls to protect yourself from getting hurt.

You can give your inner child the love, care, and understanding they may have missed. You can become the nurturing parent you always needed. This process, known as "reparenting," involves showing yourself compassion, using positive affirmations, and creating a safe, nurturing space where your inner child can thrive.

Self-compassion means treating yourself with the same kindness you'd offer a close friend. Instead of criticizing yourself for mistakes or flaws, practice self-acceptance and forgiveness. Your inner child isn't perfect, and that's okay. We all have vulnerabilities, and that's what makes us human.

Positive affirmations are like little love notes to your inner child. Replace negative self-talk with statements that remind you of your worth. Instead of saying, "I'm not good enough," try, "I am worthy of love and happiness." These simple affirmations can have a profound impact.

Creating a nurturing environment for your inner child means doing things that bring you joy, relaxation, and emotional well-being.

This could be spending time in nature, listening to music, taking a warm bath, or just enjoying a good book.

Self-care isn't selfish; it's essential for healing and growth. By nurturing your inner child, you're building a stronger emotional foundation. You're making space for your emotions to be felt and expressed, without judgment or fear.

As you continue reparenting, you might notice changes in your avoidant behaviors. You may find it easier to express your needs, be vulnerable with others, and trust in intimacy. You might even start enjoying the closeness and connection you once feared.

PROCTECTING YOUR ENERGY

Think back to the last time someone overstayed their welcome in your life, leaving you feeling drained and resentful. Maybe it was a friend who always unloaded their emotional baggage on you, a partner who ignored your needs, or a family member who crossed the line with unsolicited advice. If any of this sounds familiar, it's time to establish some boundaries.

Saying "no" can be tough, especially if you tend to avoid conflict or fear rejection. But saying "no" doesn't make you selfish; it shows that you value your time, energy, and emotional well-being. It's like telling that chatty stranger at the coffee shop, "I've got my own latte to sip and my own thoughts to think."

Imagine you're a battery, with a limited amount of energy. Every interaction, commitment, and emotional exchange draws from that energy. When you overextend yourself, you're running on empty, making yourself vulnerable to burnout and resentment. It's like trying to drive across the country on an empty tank – you might get a few miles, but it's not going to be an enjoyable trip.

Setting limits is a key part of boundary-setting. It's about deciding what you will and won't tolerate in your relationships. Think of it as putting up a "No Trespassing" sign around your heart and mind. By communicating your limits clearly, you create a safe space where your needs are respected and your energy is protected.

For example, if a coworker frequently drops by your desk to vent, instead of just gritting your teeth and enduring it, you could set a limit. Say something like, "I'm happy to chat, but I'm in the middle of something right now. Can we talk later today or tomorrow?" You're not shutting them down; you're just asserting your need for focused time.

Setting boundaries isn't always easy, especially if you're used to people-pleasing or avoiding conflict. You might face resistance or guilt trips. But remember, you're not responsible for other people's reactions. Your priority is to take care of yourself, even if it means ruffling a few feathers.

Think of it like this: you wouldn't let someone borrow your car without asking, so why let them drain your emotional energy without setting some ground rules?

Being direct and assertive is crucial when setting boundaries. Avoid vague or wishy-washy language. Instead, state your needs clearly and calmly. For instance, instead of saying, "I kind of wish you wouldn't call me so late at night," say, "I'm not available for phone calls after 9 p.m. Please text me if it's urgent."

Boundaries aren't just about saying "no." They're also about saying "yes" to the things that nourish and fulfill you. By establishing healthy boundaries, you make space for relationships, activities, and experiences that bring you joy and contribute to your overall well-being.

E

X

E

R

C

I

S

E

Write a letter to yourself from the perspective of a loving and compassionate friend. Focus on acknowledging your struggles, offering kindness and understanding, and reminding yourself of your inherent worthiness.

Objective:

The goal of this exercise is to practice self-compassion by viewing yourself through the eyes of a caring and supportive friend. This helps counteract the self-criticism and emotional distance that often accompany avoidant attachment.

Step-by-Step Instructions:

Find a Quiet Space:

- Action: Choose a comfortable and quiet spot where you won't be interrupted. This space should allow you to focus and connect with your thoughts and feelings without distractions.

Visualize a Supportive Friend:

- **Action:** Close your eyes and imagine a friend who knows you well and loves you unconditionally. This friend understands your struggles and always treats you with kindness and compassion.
- **Focus:** Picture how this friend would talk to you if they were writing a letter to support and encourage you.

Start the Letter:

- **Action:** Begin writing your letter as if you are this supportive friend. Start with a warm, caring greeting. For example, "Dear [Your Name]," or "My Dear Friend,"
- **Example:** "Dear [Your Name], I know things have been tough for you lately, and I want you to know that it's okay to feel this way…"

Acknowledge Your Struggles:

- **Action:** Gently acknowledge the challenges you've been facing, especially those related to avoidant attachment. Express understanding and empathy for these struggles.

- Example: "I see how hard it is for you to open up and trust others. You've been through a lot, and it's understandable that you protect yourself by keeping a distance..."

Offer Kindness and Understanding:
- Action: Write about how your friend (you) sees your efforts, strengths, and the progress you've made. Offer reassurance and encouragement.
- Example: "Even though you may feel distant at times, remember how strong and resilient you are. You've made it through so much, and that shows just how capable you are..."

Remind Yourself of Your Worthiness:
- Action: Emphasize that you are worthy of love, connection, and care just as you are. Remind yourself that it's okay to seek and accept support from others.
- Example: "You deserve to be loved and cared for, not just by others, but by yourself too. It's okay to let people in and trust that they care about you..."

Close with Compassionate Encouragement:

- **Action:** End the letter with a positive, hopeful message. Encourage yourself to take small steps towards self-compassion and connection with others.
- **Example:** "Take things one day at a time. Be gentle with yourself, and remember that it's okay to lean on others when you need to. You are more than enough, just as you are…"

Read the Letter Aloud:

- **Action:** After you've finished writing, read the letter aloud to yourself. Let the words sink in as if you're hearing them from a close friend. Pay attention to how it feels to receive this compassion.

Reflect on the Experience:

- **Action:** Take a few moments to reflect on how writing and reading the letter made you feel. Did it bring up any emotions? Did you notice any shifts in how you view yourself?
- **Journal:** If you'd like, jot down any thoughts or feelings that came up during the exercise.

Keep the Letter for Future Reference:

- Action: Store the letter in a safe place where you can easily find it. Revisit it whenever you need a reminder of your worth and the compassion you deserve.

How do I typically practice self-care? Are there any areas where I could be more attentive to my needs?

____

____

____

____

What activities or practices help me feel grounded, nourished, and emotionally balanced?

____

____

____

____

"*The only thing we never get enough of is love; and the only thing we never give enough of is love.*" — *Henry Miller*

Chapter 7

YOUR JOURNEY TO LOVE

The greatest thing you'll ever learn is just to love and be loved in return." Nat King Cole sang these words long ago, yet they still hold deep meaning today, especially for those seeking connection.

If you have avoidant attachment, this journey to love can feel like a winding road with unexpected detours. But remember, every twist and turn offers a chance to grow and understand yourself better.

Your story might begin in the quiet corners of childhood. Maybe a parent, though well-meaning, struggled to show affection or respond to your emotions. Or perhaps life's challenges caused disruptions in your early relationships, leaving you unsure about relying on others.

These experiences planted the seeds of avoidant attachment—a protective mechanism to keep you safe.

If love has felt unreliable or overwhelming, it makes sense that you might keep it at a distance. But this self-protection comes at a cost. The walls you've built to avoid hurt also keep out the warmth of genuine connection. The distance you maintain to protect your independence can leave you feeling isolated and lonely.

The first step in changing this pattern is understanding. Recognizing the signs of avoidant attachment in your life is like turning on a light in a dim room. Suddenly, you can see your behaviors, the triggers that activate your defenses, and the ways you might unintentionally sabotage relationships.

As you become more aware, you might notice subtle cues that signal your desire for distance. Maybe it's a sudden urge to cancel plans, focusing on your partner's flaws, or difficulty expressing your emotions.

These aren't signs of failure but opportunities for growth. Each time you catch yourself pulling away, you have a choice: you can follow old patterns or consciously choose a different path.

This journey isn't about blaming yourself or others for past hurts. It's about acknowledging your experiences, understanding their impact, and taking responsibility for your healing. It's about realizing that you deserve love and connection, even if it feels scary or unfamiliar.

The road to secure attachment may not be easy. There will be setbacks, moments of doubt, and times when old patterns resurface. But with each step forward, you'll gain confidence, resilience, and a deeper understanding of what it means to love and be loved.

EMBRACING VULNERABILITY

You've made impressive strides, haven't you? It's like finally mustering the courage to try that trendy sushi spot —nerve-wracking, but full of potential rewards.

Love, however, is no easy feat. It requires vulnerability, a feeling we avoidants often sidestep like an awkward first date. But here's a truth they don't often share in romantic comedies: vulnerability isn't a weakness; it's a superpower. It's the key to deeper connections you might have only imagined.

Look at your heart as like a fortress, built to shield you from past hurts. Those walls have protected you, but they've also kept out the sunshine. Vulnerability is like cracking open a window to let in light and warmth. Yes, it's intimidating, but it can also be exhilarating.

You might wonder, "What if I get hurt again?" It's a fair question. But the reality is, you're already feeling pain. The fortress that shields you also isolates you.

While vulnerability does involve risk, the potential for meaningful connection outweighs the potential pain.

To begin, you don't need to tear down your walls all at once. Start by inching open the gate. Share a small fear with a close friend, express a need to your partner, or simply say "I love you" without conditions.

Vulnerability isn't about over-sharing or spilling your secrets to strangers. It's about being genuine and letting yourself be seen, imperfections and all. Trust that those who appreciate your openness are the ones worth keeping, and those who don't were never meant to be in your life.

Here are some practical steps to guide you:

Start a journal. Write about your fears, dreams, and desires. It's a way to understand yourself better.

Practice self-compassion. Be gentle with yourself when things don't go as planned. Everyone makes mistakes. Seek supportive relationships. Find friends, family, or a therapist who provide a safe space for sharing.

Challenge negative self-talk. Replace thoughts like "I'm not good enough" with affirmations like "I am worthy of love." Take small steps. Focus on gradual changes rather than trying to transform everything overnight.

Think of that moment in "The Breakfast Club" when the characters open up to one another. That's the essence of vulnerability. It forges connection, understanding, and ultimately, love.

REWARDS OF SECURE ATTACHMENT

Congratulations! You've reached the final chapter of "Avoidant Attachment: Conquer the Fear of Closeness, Recognize Deactivation Signals, and Transition to Secure Attachment."

Give yourself a round of applause – you've navigated a journey that many shy away from. Seriously, you've shown tremendous bravery and dedication in understanding yourself and your relationship patterns.

Remember how we started with the origins of avoidant attachment? It was like being emotional detectives, uncovering past experiences that shaped your attachment style.

You've gained insight into why you might retreat when things get intimate, why emotional closeness can feel daunting, and why that inner critic loves to meddle with your love life.

But you didn't just stop at understanding. You took action. You learned to recognize those sneaky deactivation signals—like the sudden need for space, focusing on minor faults, or the classic "I'm fine" when you're clearly not. Identifying these signals was like discovering cheat codes to your emotional operating system.

With this new awareness, you started rewriting your relationship rulebook. You practiced expressing your needs (even when it felt like exposing your soul), improved your listening skills (goodbye, selective hearing!), and learned to handle conflict without fleeing. You even began caring for that inner child who's been holding onto past hurts. Talk about a transformation!

Now, you're not just making it through relationships – you're flourishing. You're building intimacy, fostering trust, and experiencing the kind of deep connection that once seemed reserved for movie characters (and even they have their own issues).

You've realized that vulnerability isn't a weakness; it's the secret to a fulfilling relationship.

Think of it like that scene in "When Harry Met Sally" where Harry admits his feelings for Sally. It's nerve-wracking but magical. The risk of vulnerability is worth it for the reward of deep, meaningful connection.

So, what's next? The journey doesn't end here. Secure attachment isn't a final destination; it's an ongoing process. It's like maintaining a beautiful garden—requiring constant care, weeding out negativity, and planting seeds of love and appreciation.

But you're well-equipped for the task. Keep honing your communication skills, nurturing yourself, and choosing love over fear. Each time you step outside your comfort zone, you're strengthening your secure attachment muscles. Keep going—you've come so far and have all the tools you need to continue thriving.

E
X
E
R
C
I
S
E

Write down three things you are grateful for in your relationships each day. This practice can help you cultivate a more positive and appreciative mindset, which is essential for secure attachment.

Steps:

Choose a Time:

- Action: Decide on a specific time each day when you'll do this exercise. It could be in the morning to start your day on a positive note or in the evening as a reflection before bed.

Get Your Materials:

- Action: Find a notebook, journal, or a digital note-taking app where you can write down your thoughts.

Reflect on Your Relationships:

- Action: Think about your relationships with family, friends, or partners. Consider recent interactions, moments of support, or any positive experiences you've had.

Write Down Three Things:

Action: List three specific things you are grateful for in your relationships. Be detailed to make your gratitude more meaningful. For example:

- "I'm grateful for how my friend listened to me during a tough time."
- "I appreciate the way my partner surprised me with a thoughtful gift."
- "I'm thankful for the regular check-ins from my family that make me feel supported."

Reflect on Each Item:

- Action: Spend a moment thinking about why each item on your list is important to you. How does it make you feel? How does it contribute to a positive connection with that person?

Practice Daily:

- Action: Repeat this exercise every day, adding new items to your list each time. The goal is to make this a daily habit so that over time, you naturally start focusing more on the positive aspects of your relationships.

Review and Reflect:

- **Action:** Periodically review your gratitude notes. Notice any patterns or changes in how you perceive your relationships. Reflect on how this practice might be impacting your mindset and interactions.

Optional – Share Your Gratitude:

- **Action:** If you feel comfortable, share some of your gratitude with the people involved. For example, you might tell a friend how much you appreciate their support. This can strengthen your connections and make your gratitude practice even more impactful.

What have I learned about myself and my attachment style throughout this journey?

____

____

____

____

What are my next steps in continuing to heal, grow, and cultivate secure, loving connections?

____

____

____

____

Thank You!

Congratulations on making it to the end of the workbook! I hope you found it helpful (and maybe even a little bit fun?).

Your commitment to personal growth is inspiring, and I'm grateful you chose this book to be a part of your journey.

Now, before you go, don't forget to scan the QR code below! I've got a little surprise for you—an exclusive bonus book that will help take your progress even further.

Lastly, if this workbook brought you value (or at least a few lightbulb moments), I'd love it if you could drop a review on Amazon. Your feedback helps more people discover the book—and maybe even helps them avoid the whole attachment drama thing, too.

Thanks again for trusting me with your time and growth!

"I have an everyday religion that works for me. Love yourself first, and everything else falls into line." — Lucille Ball